AF488185

"This 'companion workbook as you grieve,'
gives you Karen--a companion who is
compassionate, wise, and loyal. Karen is with
you on each and every page. She patiently sits
with you if you are too overwhelmed to turn
the page. In sacred moments, she patiently
encourages with questions, quotes, and
prompts to go deeper into the heart and soul of
your grieving."

Rev. Dr. Fran Shelton, DM
Co-Founder, Faith and Grief
Parish Associate for Caring & Belonging
First Presbyterian Church of Dallas

"This book serves as an invaluable tool for
anyone experiencing the human journey of
loss to healing. The diversity of invitations in
this book makes it relevant and accessible at
any point in time, for various types of loss."

Leonora Stephens, M.D.
Distinguished Life Fellow of the
American Psychiatric Association

Navigating Loss
with Intention

A companion workbook as you grieve

Karen Hoffman

Foreword by Alan Koenigsberg, M.D.

Navigating Loss with Intention:
A companion workbook as you grieve

Copyright ©2026
Living on Purpose

ISBN 979-8-9954095-1-9

Printed in the United States of America

Table of Contents

Table of Contents

Foreword

Karen Hoffman's new book, *Navigating Loss with Intention*, is an excellent guide for those experiencing loss.

When we think of loss, we often think first of the death of a loved one.Some losses are tangible, such as the loss of physical ability. Others are intangible, like the loss of a job or a relationship. Still others are more subtle—transitions that carry both pride and grief, such as a child leaving home.

Every loss hurts to some degree. We heal and grow when we tend to them—yet many of us don't know how. Karen Hoffman's book offers a thoughtful and practical path forward.

People process grief in different ways. Some find comfort in writing down their thoughts and feelings. Others process best through conversation, while some benefit from engaging in something more tactile or creative. Karen Hoffman honors this individuality, encouraging each reader to find what resonates and supports their own healing.

As a psychiatrist who has done extensive psychotherapy for decades, I have worked with many people experiencing all forms of loss, and I believe this book will be a meaningful and much-needed companion for those navigating loss.

Alan Koenigsberg, M.D.
Adjunct Professor of Psychiatry
University of Texas Southwestern Medical School, Dallas

Acknowledgments

 Writing this book has been a long journey. Its inception goes back to my first mentor, Sheldon Blumenthal. When I became a licensed nursing home administrator, my passion for helping people, caring for them in a holistic way, and being present as a compassionate listener, even in business environments, was cultivated by him.

During the pandemic, I started exploring mindfulness practices in creative ways. I am grateful to teachers like Michael O'Brien and Day Schildkreht. Michael's Pause-Breathe-Reflect ™ movement taught me the concept of "ripple something worth rippling." My more recent teacher, Day, founder of Morning Altars, had a transformative effect on my relationship with nature, creativity and ritual - all becoming facets of my daily life, as you'll experience yourself in the following pages. I am so grateful to both of these cherished teachers.

I've worked with many rabbis, pastors and spiritual directors who have given me strong foundations in faith, struggle, healing and wholeness. I learned new meanings of the words "loss" and "grief" beyond physically losing a loved one. That, combined with

Acknowledgments

my training as a grief group facilitator, with Faith and Grief, provided me with insights and experiences that inspired me to help others on their unique journeys through loss - individually and as a community.

My appreciation also is extended to Chris Palmore, Gratitude Space founder and author, and Gretchen Martens, Village of Care Press, write and editor extraordinaire, and friend. These two people unknowingly empowered me to see myself as a writer with something more to share than the anthologies that they invited me to contribute to.

More than any of these professional and personal connections, it is my family and dearest friends-like-family, who have inspired, motivated, and encouraged me to lean into this meaningful, personal work.

My parents have always been my greatest encouragers, for which I am forever grateful. I continue to learn from them through the various losses they have navigated with grace, love, and tenderness during all these years.

Acknowledgments

To my precious husband, Alan, my adult children and their chosen partners, whom I now consider *my* family: words cannot express my profound gratitude. Each of you has given me extraordinary encouragement in this chapter of my life: providing me the space to dream, questions to wonder about, time to write and practice in my own way, and support at every turn through this journey we share.

And finally, to those no longer here with me at this time of my life. It is the memory of these beloved family and friends that most concretely inspired me; their lives and their memories are a constant blessing. My grandparents, my brother, Steven, and my beloved friend, Wendy, are forever with me as blessings, on my own journey through grief.

Navigating my journeys through each passing, as well as other intangible losses, I discovered new ways to explore my personal grief. And now I share them with you, my readers, hopeful that you, too, can be inspired to navigate your loss with intention.

Introduction

When I was 30 years old, my brother died suddenly and unexpectedly of a heart attack. He was 26. My husband, two young sons and I lived 1500 miles away from all of our extended family. We immediately jumped on a plane - within hours of hearing the shocking and devastating news; and a new chapter of our lives began.

Thirty five years later, as a mother of three sons, I still carry and cherish the memory of that most traumatic loss of my life. All three of my own sons are now older than my beloved brother ever reached. Over time, with each subsequent loss - of grandparents, aunts, uncles, cousins, in-laws, and friends - I recognize familiar emotions and new responses to my own grief, knowing that the hole in my heart, carved out by my own loss, has influenced my life incomparably.

Sitting with a cherished friend as she died in hospice, holding space for a daughter and wife of a special friend, hearing the news of another friend's son's tragic passing, a dear friend's loss of both her father and sister within a year, and other family members and friends who have died over the past three decades, each experience of loss holds a special place in my heart.

Introduction

In 2020, as we experienced the global pandemic, I recall feeling and processing the pain of the tremendous losses we all heard about in the news. Some were personal and some were obviously distant from my own life. However, there was always a common thread that was present - each death I heard about had a griever. Somebody was always left behind to mourn the loss of a beloved human being. With my growing concern for the pain people were experiencing, I started studying, reading and learning with grief education and mindfulness professionals.

It was at the intersection of grief work and mindfulness training that I realized a companion book like this was missing for the general public: a gentle guide with concepts, activities, and reflections to guide someone on a self-paced journey.

This book may be used by people experiencing different kinds of loss - whether it's the human loss of a special person, the ending of a relationship, the loss of a cherished pet, or the grief of

Introduction

ending one chapter and moving into a new chapter of life (i.e: job change, empty-nesting, even moving). Loss is universal and the grief is often unspoken, yet present.

The more I shared the ideas and the various activities with individuals, the more I heard how helpful it would be to have the exercises, activities and reflection questions compiled in one edition.

In this book, I intentionally focus on loss more than the term "grief" because I believe that the following practices and reflection invitations are not limited to loss by a physical death. My hope is that you use this book as a companion, a guide through whatever journey of loss you are navigating. I hope that by spending time with this book, you may find new meaning in the loss you have experienced.

One question that people often ask is: What is grief and how is it connected to mourning a loss? Grief is the multifaceted response to any significant loss. While it's often associated with

Introduction

the death of a loved one - a person or a cherished pet, the loss can also be a situation that represents the ending of a chapter of our lives like a relationship or a job.

Restaurateur and renowned pasta-maker, Evan Funke, has shared about his personal journey through "professional death." In interviews and television shows, he explained that through navigating losses of restaurant closures and bankruptcy, his fears were stripped away, allowing him to enter new stages of life with a positive attitude.

Grief involves the emotional, physical and psychological response we have to loss. While mourning is the outward-facing, cultural expression of grieving a loss, grief itself involves many non-linear stages, including emotions like sadness, anger, and often guilt. Grief is experienced in waves and there is no clear timeline for how long a person grieves.

As you open this book, take a little time to reflect on the loss you are experiencing and where you are on your grief journey.

Introduction

Grief does not arrive with a map or a compass, yet each step you take moves you forward with resilience and courage.

Set aside any type of judgment or expectations. We know that grief often asks more from us than we imagine being able to carry. And yet, we all navigate loss as part of being human. Let these few moments meet you exactly where you are today - and then turn the pages to continue your personal journey.

How to use the book

Everyone's journey through loss is unique. This book is intended to be a tool that you can use at your own pace, not in a prescriptive way, but as a companion, offering opportunities to explore your grief in meaningful ways. Use it at your own pace. You can use the blank spaces and pages provided, or feel free to do your individual work in a journal or other type of notebook. You may want to revisit some of the activities multiple times.

Like grief itself, there is no "right" way to engage with this grief companion book; what matters most is that it is accessible and a meaningful experience for you.

These tips are from others who have used this book and found it useful in making meaning through the journey of grief. Feel free to modify any activity as needed for your situation, including creating new prompts or adding to what we've offered.

How to use the book

Embrace your journey through loss, using these as gentle guides that create space for reflection, connection and healing for yourself and those you love.

Honor your cherished memories and your feelings. Heal in your own time. Our intention is to help you navigate life's many types of goodbyes. Find comfort and meaning in your unique way of saying goodbye.

Whether you're grieving a beloved person, place, or part of yourself - or supporting someone else who is grieving, this self-paced book was created to hold space for experience. It is not intended to be used chronologically, in page order, or in any specific, predetermined timeline. Just as grief itself doesn't have a one-size-fits-all timeline, neither does this book have an expected timeline for completion.

How to use the book

If you flip through the book periodically, you may notice that one section, one page, one type of activity is more resonant than others. Follow your heart - let your own intuition and lived experiences guide you as you navigate your loss with intention.

Your Loss

This book begins by honoring the strength it has taken to be here today. Grief does not arrive with a map, yet each step you take reflects a quiet path toward resilience.

Before moving forward, take a few moments to reflect on the loss you experienced and where you feel you are on your grief journey today. Let your answers be honest, unfinished, and entirely your own.

Are you simply surviving each moment? Do you find brief periods of steadiness? Do you carry both sorrow and gratitude at once? Do you find yourself feeling anger? There is room here for all of it.

Your Loss

*"In order to overcome the fear,
I had to do the thing I dreaded the most."*
Evan Funke

Grief often asks more of us than we ever imagined we could carry. And yet, here you are.

Notice the loss you are carrying and the strength—visible or not—that has brought you to this moment. Consider where you are today in your grief journey, without judgment or expectation. This is your starting place.

There is no need to name what you are experiencing perfectly or move it forward. Simply notice. What feels tender? What feels heavy? What feels surprisingly steady?

Let this reflection meet you exactly where you are.

Your Loss

Name what or who you are grieving

____

____

Use your own words to describe your loss

____

____

____

Why is this loss significant to you?

____

____

____

____

Your Memories

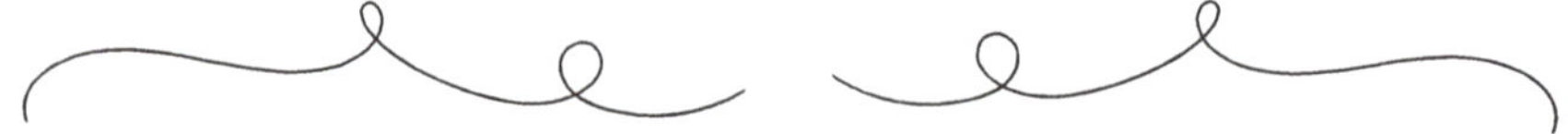

Memories are sacred. In many traditions, memory is a tool for preserving stories, sharing lived experiences, and sometimes defining who we are, based on the memory.

Through sacred memory, we honor our past, preserve experiences, heritages, and people.

We can be transformed through memory; we can honor the past, strengthen relationships with others (and ourselves), and foster our own healing.

Memories offer us a focal point for emotional healing, especially through storytelling, ritual and reflection.

Your Memories

Share a favorite memory

____

____

____

____

Share a recent memory

____

____

____

Share your oldest memory

____

____

____

Your Memories

Share a memory that makes you sad

____

____

____

____

____

Share a memory that makes you laugh

____

____

____

____

____

Your Memories

Fill in each tear drop with a memory

Feeling Grief

Where do you physically feel grief in your body?

____

____

____

What does grief feel like?

____

____

____

____

____

Feeling Grief

What do you do when your grief aches or tears at you?

____

____

____

____

When you feel angry, what do you do?

____

____

____

*"It's possible to distract ourselves to such
a degree that we avoid dealing with
anything difficult - even when our lives
would be improved by facing reality
and doing something about it."*
Marc Brackett

The Colors of Grief

*"The colors may look different now;
but they won't fade permanently."*
R.B. Kitaj

What color does grief look like to you?
Why?

____

____

____

____

____

The Colors of Grief

What emotions do colors of grief evoke in you?

____

____

____

____

____

Affirmation:
I will always feel the bright sun shining
on me - even on the darkest days.

The Colors of Grief

*"I saw the world
in black and white
instead of the vibrant colors
and shades I knew existed."*
Katie McGarry

Use this page to draw a design, in any colors that represent grief in your life.

The Colors of Grief

Use this page to draw anything,
in any colors, representing peace to you.

The Messiness of Grief

Grief is non-linear in every way: from cognitive to emotional, and even physical, There is no straight line that transports you on the journey of grief. Every person has unpredictable waves of grief that affect emotional and physical wellbeing. This is often referred to as the messiness of grief and can include anger, sadness, and many other emotions.

Use the next page to draw a similarly messy design that represents the messiness of grief to you.

Navigating the Messiness of Grief

Draw the messiness of your grief

Songs of Love and Loss

What song(s) do you
associate with this loss?

Songs of Life and Loss

How do you feel when you hear these songs now?

Songs of Life and Love

What song(s) do you
find comfort in ?

____

____

____

In what ways can music help you heal?

____

____

____

Look (to see)
Listen (to hear)
Touch (to feel)

All our human experiences are part of a journey. Along that journey, we experience both joy and laughter, love and loss. When we tap into the multiplicity of our senses, we are able to enter the healing process. Here, you are invited to look to see, listen to hear, and touch to feel, as steps along your own journey.

Do these activities outdoors, in nature, for the most meaningful experience. If you can't be outdoors, you may certainly explore indoors

Look to See

Go outside.
What does grief look like outdoors?
When you look, what do you see?

____

____

____

____

How does what you see remind
you of your loss or your healing?

____

____

____

____

Listen to Hear

Affirmation to Yourself:
*"I won't forget to listen to the
still, small voice within me."*

When you are outside, stop for at least a full minute. Listen to sounds around you.

What do you hear when you truly listen?

____

____

____

____

What is your grief saying to you?

____

____

____

____

Touch to Feel

Go outside near a tree.
Touch the tree and notice its varied textures. How does the tree's texture remind you of the grief you feel?

____

____

____

____

____

Self Care

It is critical to care for our own bodies, minds and souls. Recognizing that self-care is a necessary priority, not a selfish act, is crucial especially when grieving any type of loss.

Extending compassion to yourself is an important way to navigate your personal journey, and is a good way to model compassion to others. Asking yourself "What would help me today?" is a great first step - and the answer may be different each day, or at different times in the same day. While sometimes you may want to cry, laugh, talk with someone or be alone, it's important to recognize and prioritize self-care.

Taking gentle steps in self-care is an intentional way to navigate your loss and empowers your emotional and physical healing and resilience. These next pages include self-care tips, ideas, thoughtful prompts, and activities.

Self Care

<u>Sleep Hygiene</u>

Stay active during the day
Limit daytime naps
Spend time outdoors during the day
Maintain relaxing bedtime routine
Limit screen-time before bed
Ensure bedroom is quiet and dark
No food or drink two-hours before bed

<u>Activities for Self-Care</u>

Plant a tree or flowers in memory
Spend quiet moments, remembering
Plan a day for you, free from other duties
Notice tension in your body - release it
Collect meaningful items
Engage your senses
Listen to music
Pay attention to the present moment,
with kindness, curiosity and patience

Self Care

"Most big transformations come about from the hundreds of tiny, almost imperceptible steps we take along the way."
Lori Gottlieb

Other Ideas for Self-Care

Think of ten things that make you smile
List five things for which you're grateful
Design cards of affirmation for yourself
Adapt a positive morning routine
Consider what you've discovered that
helps when you are sad, lonely or angry
List things you are proud of right now
Acknowledge what you love about
yourself

Prioritize Self-Care

Get good sleep
Eat healthy meals
Exercise regularly
Allow yourself to feel angry and sad
Make time for enjoyable hobbies
Nurture social connections

Inside - Outside

Consider any difference between how you feel and think about grief and loss, and how you talk about grief and loss with others.
Reflect on any differences you notice.

____

____

____

____

If you notice differences, how can you ask for support you might need from others?

____

____

____

____

The Seasons

"We had joy, we had fun;
We had seasons in the sun.
But the hills that we climbed,
Were just seasons out of time."
Jacques Romain Brel

On these next few pages, spend time
associating loss with seasons.

If your grief right now was a season,
which season would it be - and why?

____

____

____

____

____

Winter

In Winter, we experience more darkness than light; and things settle quietly. How do you feel about your loss, through the dark, cold stillness of Winter?

____

____

____

____

____

*"And at the blowing of the wind, and in the
chill of winter, we remember them."*
Henry Wadsworth Longfellow

Spring

When you think of Spring, as a time of fresh new beginnings, how does that make you feel about your loss? Where do you notice softening?

Summer

Summer is often a time of play,
gathering, fun, and relaxing.
How does grief live in Summer?

Autumn

Fall is known for the release of colorful leaves, letting go of what was once part of you.

How does autumn make you think about grief and loss?

____

____

____

____

"The trees release their treasures,
each leaf a gentle prayer,
Reminding us that endings only
change the form they wear."
Heather Lea

Learning from Others

Much has been written about the grieving process, loss and healing. Here are some quotes many people find comforting and helpful at various stages of grief.

The most authentic thing about us is our capacity to create, to overcome, to endure, to transform, to love and be greater than our suffering.
Ben Okri

Don't run away from grief. Look for the remedy inside the pain because the rose came from the thorn and the ruby came from a stone.
Rumi

To live is to be willing to die - over and over again.
Pema Chodron

Should you shield the valleys from the windstorms, you would never see the beauty of their canyons.
Elisabeth Kubler-Ross

"Death steals the future we anticipated and hoped for, but it can't take away the relationship we had."
Julia Samuel

Your grief path is yours alone. No one else can walk it, and no one else can understand it.
Terri Irwin

Learning from Others

*"The purpose of learning is growth.
Our minds, unlike our bodies, continue
growing as we continue to live."*
Mortimer Adler

Use this space to write any of your own favorite quotes that you've encountered on your journey.

Some people enjoy making a set of index cards of collected quotes to use in the future.

Jar of Rocks

A teacher walks into a classroom, setting a glass jar on the table. He places large rocks in the jar until no more can fit. He asks the class if the jar is full and they agree it is. He replies, "Really?" and grabs a pile of small pebbles, adding them to the jar, shaking it slightly until they fill the spaces between the rocks.

He asks again, "Is the jar full?" They agree it is. Next, he adds a scoop of sand to the jar, filling the space between the pebbles, asking the question again. This time, the class is divided, some feel that the jar is obviously full, but others are wary of another trick.

Grabbing a pitcher of water, he fills the jar to the brim, saying, "If this jar is your life, what does this experiment show you?" A bold student replies, "No matter how busy you think you are, you can always take on more."

"That's one view," the teacher replies. "The rocks represent BIG things in your life: what you will value at the end of life - family, friends, health, fulfilling your hopes and dreams. The pebbles are other things that give your life meaning: your job, house, hobbies, casual friendships. The sand and water represent the 'small stuff' that fills our time: watching TV or running errands."

Looking at the class again, he asks, "Can you see the difference if I lead with the sand and pebbles?"

Jar of Rocks

Based on the story, imagine this is your jar of rocks. Identify "big rocks" that guide your life. Label the big rocks in this jar. Think about your pebbles and sand. Consider how you make time for the big and small rocks in life.

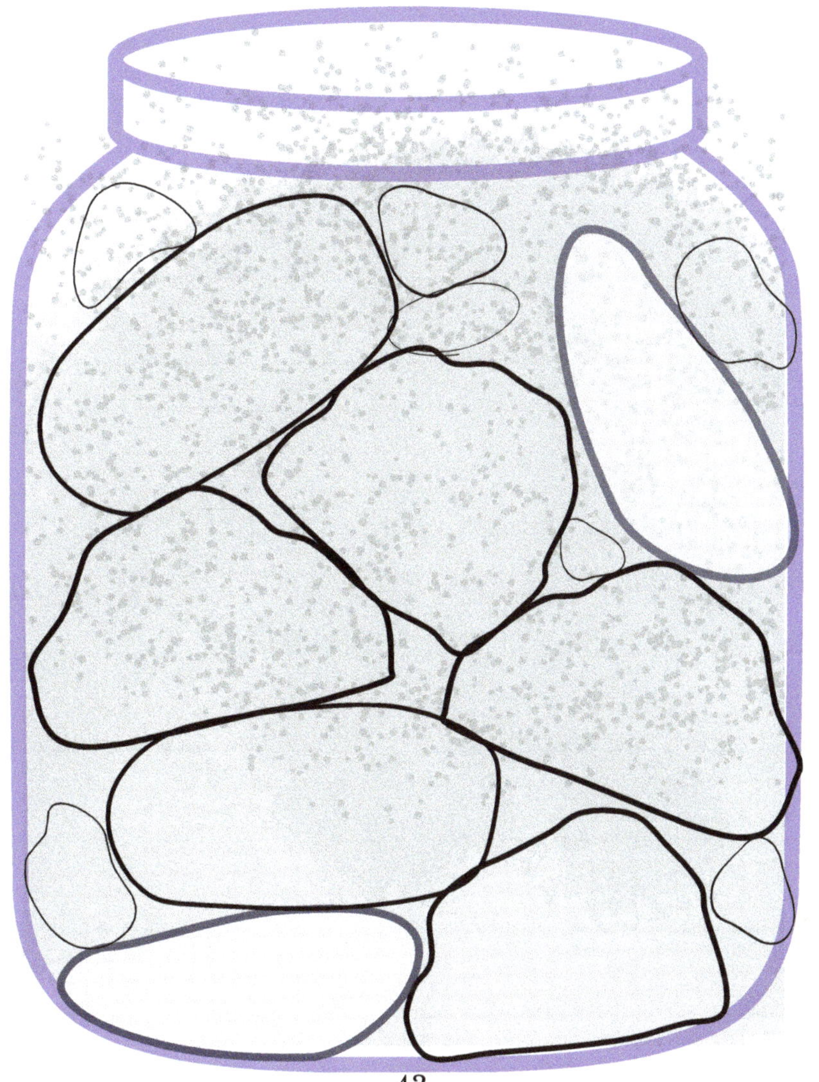

Jar of Rocks

Think about your big rocks, pebbles and sand. How does your loss impact your jar of rocks?

____

____

____

____

How do you make space and time in your life for both the big and small things that matter, when you are grieving?

____

____

____

Backpack of Grief

Imagine you have a backpack full of grief and loss. What is taking up space in the backpack? Do feelings like anger, sadness and regret weigh you down? What would you like to release, to lighten the heaviness of the backpack you carry? What might each release feel like?

Kintsugi

"I know exactly where my cracks are and how deep they run ... the truth is, we are all broken in places."
C. JoyBell C.

Kintsugi is an ancient Japanese art form of repairing cracks in a vessel and sealing the cracks with gold. It can be a useful and beautiful metaphor for grief, with many lessons about life:

- Embracing imperfections
- Focusing on the journey of repair
- Honoring the process
- Finding beauty in the brokenness
- Healing brokenness without hiding

Using the process of Kintsugi, we can focus on resilience, rebuilding and accepting something we love in a different way than it once was.

On the next page, you will have an opportunity to explore the art of Kintsugi with your grief.

Kintsugi

- In this space, draw a bowl or another pottery item.
- Add some cracks, widening the cracks with a double line.
- When you have drawn the cracks, fill in the cracks with words that represent broken-ness in you.
- Then, cover the cracks with a gold marker or paint, beautifying the piece, knowing the cracks still exist.

What patterns or themes arose in you?

____

____

What did you feel as you named, created and then wrote in the cracks - filling them?

____

____

Niksen

Niksen is the Dutch "art of doing nothing." Practicing Niksen can be a wellness activity, intentionally doing something without purpose. This type of purposeful idleness reduces anxiety, while often boosting creativity and productivity.

Reflect on what it might feel like to give yourself permission to lean into "doing nothing," being wherever you are, doing what you need, even allowing yourself to feel overwhelmed by what's ahead of you?

____

____

____

What other ways can you imagine taking a break from thoughts that focus on your loss? How can you use purposeful idleness when you feel overwhelmed?

____

____

____

Niksen
Purposefully Doing Nothing

"Within you, there is a stillness and a sanctuary to which you can retreat at any time and be yourself."
Hermann Hesse

We tend to say "yes" to so many things that fill our calendars and our days. What does it feel like to just sit and stare at a blank page? What do you notice? How do you feel? Imagine ways that this can help you when your thoughts turn to grief?

Kaizen

Kaizen is a Japanese philosophy of taking small, continuous steps toward improvement or healing, instead of focusing on "getting over" something. Practicing Kaizen, we incrementally move forward on our journey through grief.

<u>Introducing Kaizen to Grief Work</u>

- Take a little step: When you're overwhelmed by grief, focus on a little action - even if it's simply going outside for 5 minutes.
- Be kind to yourself: Acknowledge that this is a long process that requires patience.
- Celebrate small wins: Recognize that even small actions are moving you forward in a positive way.

What small steps can you take on your journey through loss, even just one thing?

____

____

____

____

Writing

Did you know that research shows that writing through emotional experiences can boost your physical immunity and mood? Expressive writing can help you make sense of loss, helping you gain new insights, and process what you're going through. Below are some sample writing prompts you may want to use. Spend between 5-15 minutes on each one, over a period of weeks.

What grief reactions are most uncomfortable for you and why?

When does anger appear and what might its message be for you?

What qualities did they bring into your life that you still carry?

What was something ordinary that you shared that now feels sacred?

What is something you wish others understood about your grief?

Write about a time when your grief surprised you.

Writing

Write a letter of compassion from your future self (any time in the future) to you now.

What does *"moving forward"* mean to you? (**not** *moving on*)

Write about one hope you have for yourself in the next month. What about next year?

What moments make you wish you could be with them the most?

If your grief could talk, what would it say?

Write about one thing you never want to forget about them.

Write about one small thing that brought you comfort today.

If your goal is not "to get over it," write about what your goal could be.

Where does your mind go when you let it wander?

What is something you wish your support system understood about your grief journey?

What are three ways that your support system can help you?

Mandalas for Healing

"Each person's life is like a mandala - a vast, limitless circle. We stand in the center of our own circle, and everything we see, hear and think forms the mandala of our life."

Pema Chödrön

Mandala (Sanskrit) is considered a 'sacred circle.' You do not need to have artistic skill to create a mandala, only a desire to explore as you move through your journey of loss and grief.

For this activity, you may want a piece of paper, as well as something circular to use as a template, and some colored pencils, pens or markers.

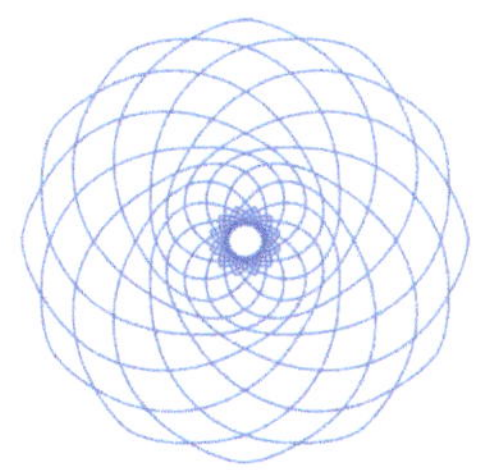

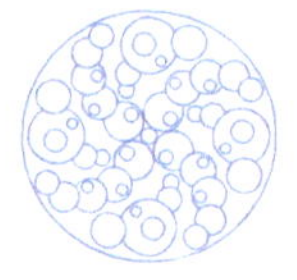

Guidelines for Creating Mandalas

"The mandala is a map for spiritual transformation."
Tsultrim Allione

- Relax and take a few deep breaths, inhaling through your nose and exhaling through your mouth or nose. Repeat a few times.
- Notice if anything feels uncomfortable. If so, try to ease into the discomfort. Next, notice any colors or shapes that come to you. This can be the starting point for your mandala. If you don't sense anything, that is okay, too.
- Open your eyes if they were closed.
- Choose a color to start with.
- Draw a circle, using a circular template.
- Don't overthink what you're doing.
- Begin to fill in your circle with color and shapes of any kind. Or you can extend beyond the circle.

Typically, it's easiest to begin at the center and work outward or begin at edges, working inward. Spend as much time as you want doing this.

Space to Create
Your Own Mandala

Give yourself time to look at your creation. What can you learn from the process, and the mandala you created, that can be a lesson in your personal grief journey?

____

____

____

____

Creating Rituals in Nature

Bringing nature, ritual, and creativity together is often a meaningful process in contemplative work, especially healing and grief. While there are many ways you can cultivate your own rituals, here are some practices you may try in various seasons.

"Nature, art, and ritual are ways that cultures around the world have been transforming grief into beauty for thousands of years. Separately, these three things can open our hearts, bring us back to our center, and connect us back into what's meaningful. Together, they become a resource and skill so we can feel human again."

Day Schildkret, _Morning Altars_

Creating Rituals in Nature

Creating impermanent art outdoors, with beautiful treasures found in nature, allows us to:

- Process emotions - relating to a personal experience
- Make meaning - honoring and remembering
- Embrace impermanence - connecting ever-changing nature to human life
- Cultivate flexibility - building resilience while facing change
- Inspire curiosity - creating a sense of awe and wonder

What is your relationship to nature?

____

____

____

____

Creating Rituals in Nature

- Take a walk outside, collecting items in nature like leaves, branches, petals and rocks.
- Pause in a place that feels comfortable.
- Think about a facet of your loss such as the memory of an experience you shared or some aspect of your grief itself.
- Use that thought as inspiration as you take your nature finds and place them into a design that will be left behind as you walk away.
- When your nature art feels complete, reflect on your emotions, the process, any feelings that come up and your responses.
- Before leaving, take a photo of your creation, and say or write down a blessing, a sentence, or a reminder

____

____

Morning Altars is a 7-step process combining nature, ritual and creativity. To learn more, see resource section in the back of this book.

Affirmations

Affirmation statements can help us rewire negative thought patterns, as we focus on the positive in the present-tense

Try using any of these on a regular basis. Then, make up your own when you're comfortable. Consistent repetition will boost self-esteem, increase confidence, promote clarity, and improve overall well-being by shifting perspective and influencing brain activity in positive ways.

- *I allow myself to feel this pain fully and without resistance.*
- *It's okay to grieve; and I can give myself the time and space I need.*
- *I am gentle with myself as I heal.*
- *My emotions are valid and powerful.*
- *I am strong, capable of moving forward.*
- *I am learning to discover a new me.*
- *I am grateful for the time I shared with my loved one.*
- *I can feel anger, regret and sorrow. along my journey.*
- *I will honor their memory by living fully.*
- *I am surrounded by support, both seen and unseen.*
- *I can accept help*
- *I can feel and see the love in the world.*
- *I am grateful for my memories.*

Facing Fears

Grief experts like David Kessler and Julia Samuel teach that feeling and facing fear are important elements of coping with loss. Similarly, Evan Funke navigated a journey of "professional death," teaching us the same lessons.

As you approach the last exercises in this book, take some time to name your fears and use some of your new tools to identify ways to cope with them.

How has this loss left you feeling afraid?

Facing Fears

What are you most afraid of because of your loss?

____

____

____

____

What small steps can you take to confront or start to overcome your fears?

____

____

____

____

Stepping into Hope

"In any given moment, we have two options: to step forward into growth or step back into safety."
Abraham Maslow

Consider a time when you felt a sense of safety. Describe that feeling with words or drawings.

Stepping into Hope

*"Grief is like the ocean;
it comes in waves, ebbing and flowing.
Sometimes the water is calm, and sometimes it is
overwhelming. All we can do is learn to swim."*
Vicki Harrison

Like a crashing wave, sometimes our safety is suddenly shaken, and we feel unsettled.

Consider a time when your safety was shaken. How did your body respond? Write or draw about it.

Stepping into Hope

*"People say grief comes in waves.
What you don't know until you're in grief is that
those waves come crashing in. And the other thing
no one tells you is the waves never really stop.
But in time, if you're lucky, you learn to float."*
David Kessler

In the turbulence of grief, what emotions do you feel strongly, undercutting your sense of safety and security? Write them into the waves.

Then, look at the waves you've filled and write about how that feels and what you can do to feel more comfortable today.

Stepping into Hope

Notice the waves you've filled on the previous page. Write about how that feels.

____

____

____

____

What can you do to feel safer and more comfortable today?

____

____

____

____

Connect the Dots

Remember connect-the-dots?
In childhood, many people make
designs by connecting the dots
in sequential order. Try it here.

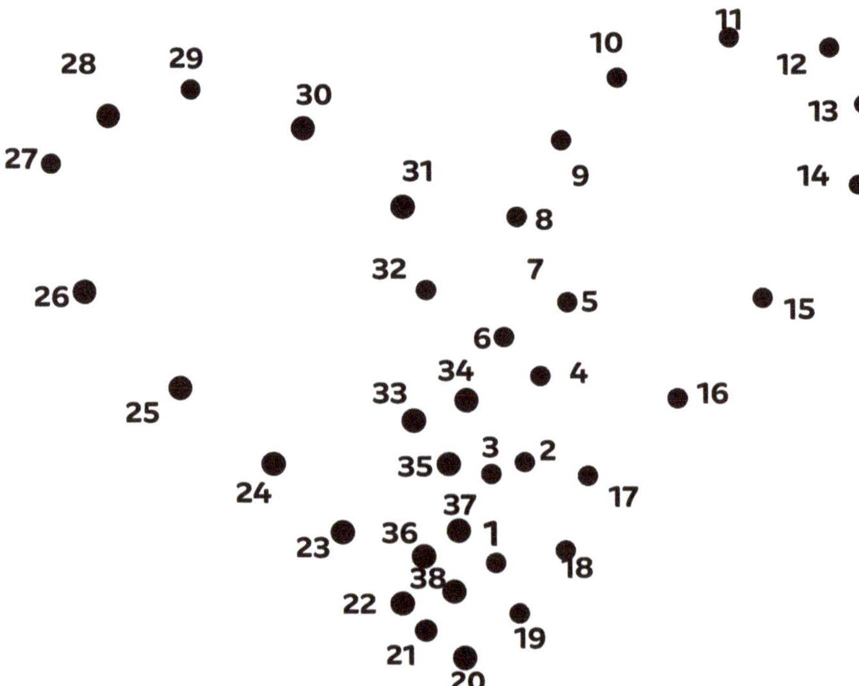

Next, as you make your way through the
messiness of your grief, you won't be
using the numbers as training wheels.
You're doing it yourself.

Connecting the Dots

In the space below, draw 36 dots.
They can be clustered together or
symmetrically lined-up. You can place
them randomly or intentionally.
There is no wrong way to place your dots.

Connecting the Dots

Connect your dots from the previous page.

Pick one dot and connect to another dot in a line. Then, continue moving so that eventually each dot is connected to at least one other dot. There are no other rules.

It's not going to look like a perfect connect-the-dot from a coloring book. The important thing is to connect to what you're doing - not what you're imagining to create as an outcome. This is fearless exploration - without training wheels.

Consider what emotions arose during the process. How did you feel when connecting the first dots? How did your energy change as you continued? How did your body respond? What thoughts came to you?

____

____

____

____

Removing the Training Wheels

Removing training wheels is usually scary. Yet it is necessary for growth as you learn to ride a bike. The same is true as you navigate your journey through grief.

Training Wheels of Grief

Aftermath of Grief
Feeling scared, sad, angry, unsettled, unstable

Wobbling and Wondering
Perceiving you're unstable, sometimes wondering if you're making progress

Finding New Balance
Sensing you're unsteady as you practice moving forward, finding independent balance

Removing the Training Wheels
Knowing the terrain is always challenging *and* that you can do this thing called life after loss

Resources

Books on Grief

Camille Sapara Barton, *Tending Grief*

Joanne Cacciatore, *Bearing the Unbearable*

Megan Devine, *It's O.K. that You're Not O..K.*

Jack Jordan & Bob Baugher, *After Suicide Loss: Coping with your Grief*

David Kessler, *Finding Meaning*

Elisabeth Kubler-Ross, *On Grief & Grieving*

Harold Kushner, *When Bad Things Happen to Good People*

Steve Leder. *The Beauty of What Remains*

Steve Leder. *More Beautiful than Before*

Naomi Levy, *To Begin Again*

C. S. Lewis, *A Grief Observed*

Jan Warner, *Grief Day by Day*

Nisha Zenoff, *The Unspeakable Loss: How do you live after a child dies?*

Resources

Books on Practices, Rituals, and Grief

Patti Digh, ***The Geography of Loss***
Robert Maurer, ***Kaizen: One Small Step Can Change Your Life***
Annette Laurijsen, ***Niksen, The Dutch Art of Doing Nothing***
Day Schildkret, ***Hello, Goodbye***
Day Schildkret, ***Morning Altars***
Fran Tilton Shelton, ***The Spirituality of Grief: Ten Practices for Those Who Remain***
Elana Zaiman, ***The Forever Letter***

Grief Resources, Websites, and Support Groups

"All There Is" - Anderson Cooper's Podcast
CompassionateFriends.org
FaithandGrief.org
Good-Grief.org
Grief.com
Griefshare.org
TheDinnerParty.org

www.ingramcontent.com/pod-product-compliance
Lightning Source LLC
Chambersburg PA
CBHW040733120726
48010CB00002B/99